Level 2

The Nature Kid's Guide to

PENGUINS

RENATA MARIE

LP Media Inc. Publishing

For information address LP Media Inc. Publishing,
3178 253rd Ave. NW, Isanti, MN 55040
www.lpmedia.org

Publication Data

Penguins
The Nature Kid's Guide to Penguins — First edition.

Summary: "Learn all about Penguins, the Nature Kid Way"
— Provided by publisher.

ISBN: 978-1-954288-69-0

[1. Penguins - Non-Fiction] I. Title.

Title: The Nature Kid's Guide to Penguins

CONTENTS

ICY LIVING

Ice floats over the sea. Snow falls. A King penguin waddles and slides.

Most penguins live in Antarctica. It is the coldest place on Earth. It can be −128 degrees Fahrenheit (−89 degrees Celsius). The cold winds can reach 200 miles (322 kilometers) per hour.

Penguins live on the ice. They swim in the cold waters. And they **huddle** together in snow storms.

DID YOU KNOW?

There are 18 types of penguins. Some live where it is warm.

BIG BIRDS

Wind blasts an Emperor penguin. But he stands tall.

Emperor penguins are the biggest type of penguin. They are one of the largest birds on Earth. They are four feet (1.2 meters) tall. They weigh up to 100 pounds (45 kilograms). Male penguins are a bit bigger than females.

FUN FACT! A long time ago, there was a giant type of penguin. It was over five feet (1.5 m) tall.

FLUFFY FEATHERS

FUN FACT!

Emperor penguins can have up to 1.6 inches (4.1 centimeters) of fat around their bodies.

A Chinstrap penguin waddles over the ice. His fat keeps him warm.

Penguins stay warm even in the coldest weather. Fat in their bodies keeps them warm.

They have two sets of feathers. The feathers close to their bodies are fluffy. They trap air; that keeps the penguins warm. **Their feathers also keep out the wind and water.**

They even have feathers on their legs to keep them warm.

When it is really cold, penguins tuck their wings close to their bodies. They shiver to make heat.

FLYING UNDER-WATER

Splash! A Gentoo penguin dives into the ocean.

Penguins cannot fly in the sky. **But they can fly in the water.** Their bodies are shaped to slide easily through the water. Their wings look like **flippers**. They flap them up and down. They push through the water. Their feet are webbed. They use them to turn.

Penguins can swim 8.9 miles (14 km) per hour. They can stay under the water for more than 20 minutes. They dive deep to find food.

DID YOU KNOW?

One time, a penguin dove 1850 feet (564 m) deep. That is deeper than the Empire State Building is tall!

GONE FISHING

A Humboldt penguin peers into the blue. Silver flashes—a fish!

Penguins swim in the ocean to find food. Each of their eyes has a clear eyelid. It lets them see under the water. **They can easily spot prey.**

Penguins dive at prey. Pointy tips on their bills catch the food. Pointy bumps on their tongues keep the food from slipping out. And the penguins swallow their food whole. Even while swimming.

FUN FACT!

Penguins do not have teeth.

PENGUIN PREY

Snap! A penguin is on the hunt.

Penguins are **carnivores**. **They eat meat.** They eat fish. They eat krill and squid. Each day, they eat up to 13.2 pounds (6.0 kg) of food. They eat a lot so they can build up fat. They need a lot of fat for the cold winters.

Squid

Krill

Herring

FUN FACT!

One time, a penguin stayed under the water for 32 minutes. That is a long time!

SCARY TEETH

Antarctic Skuas

Giant Petrels

Killer Whale

Leopard Seal

The ocean grows dark. A Leopard seal swims above a penguin.

Large animals with teeth swim in the ocean. **Penguins have to keep an eye out for predators.** Leopard seals, Killer whales and large birds hunt them.

When they spot a predator, penguins race for the ice. They let bubbles out of their feathers. The bubbles form a tunnel of air. It makes the water easier to swim through.

The penguins jump out of the water and land safely on the ice.

DID YOU KNOW?

Bubbles help penguins swim up to three times faster.

FANCY FEATHERS

The penguin swims under the seal. But the predator does not spot her.

Penguins use camouflage to hide from predators. Their black backs look like the deep ocean. **Their white bellies look like the bright sun.**

They also use their feathers to keep warm. They turn their backs toward the sun. Their black feathers warm up quickly.

FUN FACT!

A penguin's camouflage also helps it hide from prey.

WADDLE WADDLE

An Emperor penguin jumps out of the water. He slides and waddles away.

Penguins move smoothly in the water. **But on land, they waddle.** They can only walk at 1.5 miles (2.4 km) per hour.

Sometimes they need to go faster. They slide on their bellies. They use their wings to pull. They use claws on their feet to push. They can slide for miles.

DID YOU KNOW?

A type of penguin can hop on rocks. They are called Rockhoppers.

CLIFF CLIMBERS

A Gentoo penguin walks up a cliff. The ice is slippery, but he keeps climbing.

Penguins can walk up cliffs. The cliffs are icy. But penguins dig their claws into the ice. They stick their **bills** into the snow.

The ice near the ocean can melt. Penguins want to have their babies in a safe place. The ice has to last until the babies are old enough to swim.

FUN FACT!

Sometimes penguins get cold feet. They tip back on their tails and lift their toes off the ice.

PARENT PENGUINS

A female penguin lays an egg. She rolls it onto the feet of the father.

Penguins live in groups called **colonies**. **There can be thousands of penguins in a colony.**

When winter comes, female penguins go fishing. They are hungry after laying eggs. The fathers stay with the eggs.

DID YOU KNOW?

A group of penguins in the water is called a raft. A group of penguins on land is called a waddle.

FROZEN FATHERS

Snow flies over the ice. A group of King penguins huddle for warmth. Each holds an egg.

Father penguins hold their eggs on their feet. They keep their eggs warm in their feathers.

In Antarctica, the sun does not rise in the winter. It is dark. It is cold.

The males huddle close to keep warm. The center of the huddle is warm. Each penguin takes a turn on the outside, where the snowstorms blow.

DID YOU KNOW?

Penguin chicks take two months to come out of their eggs.

CUTE CHICKS

FUN FACT!

Groups of penguin chicks are called crèches. That means "crib."

The sun warms the ice. An egg breaks open. A little face peeks out.

Baby penguins are called chicks. They only weigh about seven ounces (198 grams) when they are born. They stay warm in their fathers' feathers. They chitter and chirp.

Chicks call to other chicks still in their eggs. They want them to come out of their eggs. This way, all of the chicks come out together.

The chicks open their mouths for food. Their fathers have not eaten in months. But they throw up what they can. Luckily, the chicks' mothers come home.

COMING HOME

FUN FACT!

As penguins grow older, their parents leave them in crèches. The adults go fishing.

A mother penguin waddles over the rocks. She calls for the father penguin.

Each penguin looks the same. But they each have their own call.

The penguins call. They find each other. **And the mothers meet their chicks for the first time.** They feed their chicks. They watch over them. And the fathers go fishing.

Over a few months, the chicks will grow taller. They lose their baby feathers. They grow adult feathers. And they will also get to go fishing.

SCARIER THAN TEETH

A penguin swims. He watches for predators. But he does not see the oil.

There are many Emperor penguins. **But many could die if nothing changes.** And soon.

There are 650,000 Emperor penguins in the wild. But they still face dangers. And the dangers can be scarier than predators.

DID YOU KNOW?

Some types of penguins are close to dying out. There are only 3,000 Yellow-eyed penguins left.

MELTING HOME

Ice melts. It breaks away. Penguins are losing their homes.

The Earth is warming. The ice around Antarctica is melting. Some penguins never live on land. They only live on sea ice.

Less ice means fewer safe places. They will not have space to make more eggs. They will not have a home for their chicks. They will be closer to hungry predators in the sea.

KIDS CAN HELP THE EARTH

- Turn off computers
- Unplug chargers
- Take shorter showers

SWIMMING IN TRASH

A penguin tries to swim, but something sticks to her feathers.

People throw trash in the ocean. It can hurt penguins. It can make it hard for them to swim. But trash is not the only danger.

Sometimes oil spills into the ocean. Penguins swim through it. It makes them sick. It sticks to their feathers. It makes it hard to float. It makes it hard to hunt. It makes it hard to stay warm.

DID YOU KNOW?

People try to save birds from oil spills. They clean the ocean. They wash the oil off the birds.

EMPTY OCEAN

A fish flashes past. A penguin chases it. But a net catches the fish.

People use big nets to catch fish and krill. They catch a lot of sea animals. There is less and less food for penguins. If they cannot catch food, they will go hungry. Their chicks will go hungry.

People are trying to help penguins. They made safe places for penguins where there are no fishing boats. There are no oil spills. Penguins are free to hunt and swim.

FUN FACT!

There are about 66 Emperor penguin colonies.

GLOSSARY

bills
the beak of the penguin that opens and closes their mouth
page 23

carnivores
animals that eat meat
page 15

colonies
groups of penguins who live together
page 25

flippers
parts of animals used to swim
page 11

huddle
to stand close together
page 5

waddle
to walk with short steps
page 21

MORE AMAZING ANIMAL BOOKS from Nature Kids Publishing!

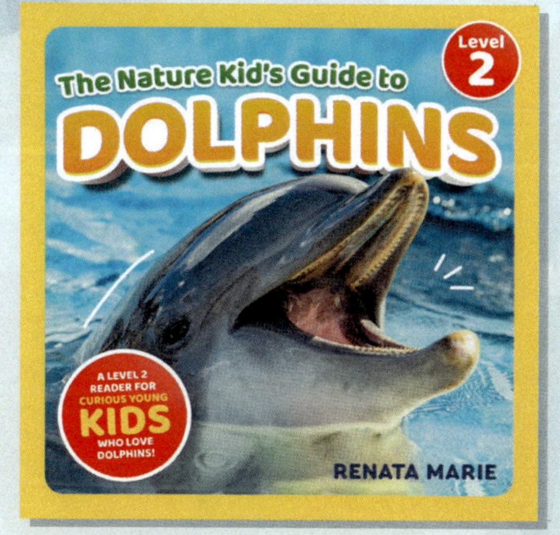

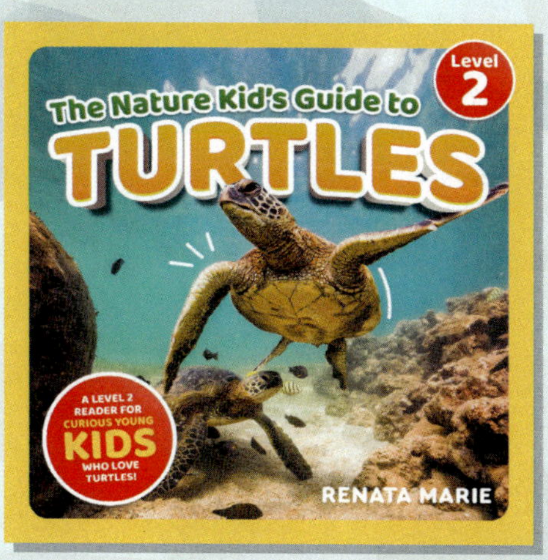

The Nature Kid's Guide to
Level 2
LIONS
A LEVEL 2 READER FOR CURIOUS YOUNG KIDS WHO LOVE LIONS!
RENATA MARIE

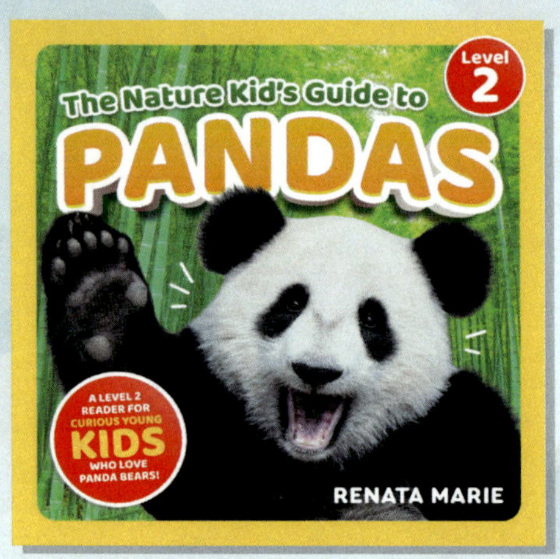
The Nature Kid's Guide to
Level 2
PANDAS
A LEVEL 2 READER FOR CURIOUS YOUNG KIDS WHO LOVE PANDA BEARS!
RENATA MARIE

The Nature Kid's Guide to
Level 2
OWLS
A LEVEL 2 READER FOR CURIOUS YOUNG KIDS WHO LOVE OWLS!
RENATA MARIE

The Nature Kid's Guide to
Level 2
MEERKATS
A LEVEL 2 READER FOR CURIOUS YOUNG KIDS WHO LOVE MEERKATS!
RENATA MARIE

Made in the USA
Las Vegas, NV
20 August 2023

76364384R00026